One Month

David Flynn

Cyberwit.net
HIG 45 Kaushambi Kunj, Kalindipuram
Allahabad - 211011 (U.P.) India
http://www.cyberwit.net
Tel: +(91) 9415091004
E-mail: info@cyberwit.net

Hamster, Hammurabi, hammer.
Ham.
I am not sure why those occur to me this morning,
but they do.
Such is my mind.
Such is your mind,
especially if you are reading this.
Marco Polo. Polo shirt. Mark my words.
Mark.
Marker. Market. Marsupial.
Mar.
I could go on all day.
This is fun.
But maybe not for you.
Words connect and they disconnect.
Hamster, Teamster.
Marco Polo, pony.
We think all day, two three four.
Then there is a noise outside the window:
squirrel.
Then squirrel, bushy tale, squirrel stew at my great-aunt's,
squirrel away my salary, squirrel eating a nut, squirrel acrobats in
the trees,
squire, pyre, fire, ghost chilis.
So that when I try to decide on an issue like 'Is there an after-
life?"
I pun.
Sun, fun, ghost, host, die, why, heaven, leaven, hell, bell,
and get nowhere.
Systems are made like this: existentialism, capitalism, Naziism.
But they rule our lives, inter-human.

Squirrels, they care less.
Nuts,
that's what's important to them.
Seeds.
Really I don't know what's important to squirrels,
I just know nuts and seeds,
juts and weeds,
butts and steeds.

I am lost but so is Wittgenstein.
Bit, ten, mine.
So is the pope,
so is the Putin,
so is the Trump,
so is the bump,
so is the hump,
so is the sump pump.

I am lost.

So it starts, this poetry journal.
Maybe I'll get more sleep tonight.
Maybe not.
A sample.
An ample sample.

September 11, 2022

Brain winds.
And this is what my brain winds blow in today:
leaves.
The autumn of creation.
Aren't metaphor, simile, symbols, comparisons wonderful?
Without them we would be stuck with reality.
The desk, the lamp, the computer, my fingers, the keyboard.
Those things would mean nothing.
Wait.
Maybe they do mean nothing.
But let's say the desk is symbolic of civilization.
Desks don't grow in fields;
they are manufactured,
which implies a vast system of transportation, employment,
science, and society.
More more more than that.
So let's call it the desk of destiny.
I am here.
It is here.
We were destined to be together.
The desk holds my computer, sheets of paper, my coffee cup,
and many other items,
and thus represents
a sample of my work life.
The Desk of Destiny.
That's better.

Brain winds.
Some days they are breezes.
Some days they are storms.

Some days they are still.
Brain rain.

September 12, 2022

A new day,
But all days are old.
In a lifetime maybe three days are different,
maybe four,
maybe five.
Different good I mean.
Different bad add another five or more.
Thousands the same.
So today is Monday.
Blue skies, cool,
the same.
We blow up our lives like balloons.
Mine is red, I think, but ordinary size.
A string keeps it tied to a chair,
maybe.
Metaphor again.
One day pop.
But heah, in the meantime,
I can eat a good lunch,
a cookie or two for fun,
Zoom,
read my current book more,
drink a glass of wine.
Sleep.
The usual because today is not new.
I can't complain.
To whom?
To what?
For what?
Make my life a series of exciting, important days,
365 days a year,

1 more in Leap Years.
Every day new; every day surprising and an achievement.
That would be exhausting.
Mostly I want old days, but more new ones.
Not a lot but more.
Then death.

I hope this isn't too depressing.
It just is.
Happy Old Year.
Happy Old Day.
For me.
For you.
The best
that can be.

Blue sky isn't that bad,
Neither are cookies.

September 13, 2022

Rumba, cha cha cha, Charleston, waltz, minuet, Bunny Hop,
Flamenco, disco, Gangnum style,
hula, jig, line, Lambada, mashed potato, Morris, square, shimmy,
slow, twist, tango, Watusi, YMCA, hip
hop, moonwalk, twerking.
Just a sample of what we humans have done with our bodies.
More dances, almost, than religions.
The nuns taught us how to waltz with a ruler's length between
male and female.
The Gator: lie prone on the floor and hunch.
The Macarena.

I think I'm a good dancer, but my wife doesn't.
She kept telling people how jerky I am until I had a t-shirt made.
Black with a white cartoon of a dancer on the front, and the
words
"I INHABIT THE GROOVE."
That tells her.

In Japan everybody on the floor danced with the others, no two-
somes, or
danced with themselves, looking at the mirrors on the dance floor
wall.

Ballet of course and modern, but that's not what I am talking
about.

Holding you close I feel your body next to mine.
Fast dance, separate, fast dance, separate, fast dance, separate,
then,

thank goodness,
slow dance.
Put your arms around my neck.
Warmth.
Shape.
Two as one.

I miss dancing.
Haven't been dancing in 30 years.
But I still inhabit the groove.

September 14, 2022

I have several superstitions,
like Sept. 13.
It's over now.
Good.
Whew.
Survived that one.
Now it's the 14th, a clearer day.
And 4's.
In Japan 4 is a bad number because
shi means 4 and death.
Avoid 4's.
In America we don't like 13's.
I could look up why, but why?
So September 13, October 13, it happens every month.
And somehow I don' like zeroes,
so that when I read I try not to stop on a page with a zero,
Like 200 but even 202, 204, 206, etc.

Some of this I picked up in graduate school studying the Middle
Ages.
3 was good, the trinity.
9 was best, a trinity of trinities.
Numerology.
Jewish kabbalah.
I knew a man in Mitze Roman, Israel,
where I had a writing residency.
He was a Russian émigré, mostly working construction for
survival,
but on the side he drew enormously complicated, beautiful charts
of numbers,
kabbalah.

From him I learned that 666 was a numerological equivalent of Nero,
and that Nero was persecuting Jews.
So 666 was bad.
Once I checked out a few groceries, milk, bread, odds and ends.
When the total came to $6.66 the clerk freaked.
She wouldn't let me pay that.
In fact, she put a dollar and some change of her own into the payment,
so that I had to pay $4 and something.
Then she relaxed.
No 666.

My 13th birthday. I don't remember it.
My 44th birthday. I don't remember it.
My 66th birthday. I don't remember it.
My 444th birthday. Yeah, right.

So happy 1 and 3 and 9.
In Japan 8 is the lucky number; I'm not sure why.
So happy 8.
Another superstition I have.
Doesn't have to be in a graveyard.
11:13 a.m. 12:13 p.m.
Can't be avoided.

Numbers are real as bricks.
To me. Superstitions are bricks too. I act based on them.
Hug the good numbers; kick the bad numbers; enjoy the others
because they are, well,
numerous.

September 15, 2022

Noise.
White noise.
Chartreuse noise.
Scarlet noise.
Gray noise.
Plaid noise.

A motor rumbles outside.
Would be good to sleep to.

Sound, next to sight, is my favorite sense.
The sound of her voice.
The sound of bacon frying in a pan.
The sound of a choir.
The sound of a blues singer.
The sound of the wind in the trees.

Too bad we have only five senses.
We don't know what else there is out there.
If we had six senses, seven senses, a hundred senses,
there might be civilizations in the front yard.
We just don't know.
To touch we have to put our fingers, elbows, something, on the
thing.
To taste we have to put the thing in our mouths.
That's not strong.
That's not useful.
Touch the universe.
Taste God.
But
smell love.

Yes, skin, perfume.
Taste love.
Yes, skin, lips.
Limited, but they help.

The sight of this computer screen.
Ah.
The sight of rain falling on the sky light.
The sight of a plate full of scrambled eggs.
Yes.

Five senses.
They are our contact with the world outside our skins.
Everything else, thoughts, are in our brain.
Jars using legs to sense new places.
That's us.
Even reading is impossible without sight.
Or sound if being read to.
Or touch if braille.
Taste and smell don't count here.

I am glad I am human
But there are alternatives.

September 16, 2022

Evren, my grandson, is 1.
1 year.
1 person.
1 wonder.

A gap because I drove 300 miles to Evren's first birthday party, and was gone for two days.

September 19, 2022

So much to write about:
my grandson's first birthday,
my ex-wife at the party,
family,
bed bugs at the motel and a body full of red blisters.
But
there's a cat in the room.
She ran around my legs when I opened the door to the stairs.
Now she is here meowing, meowing, meowing,
Running around.
I can't write with her in the room.
I have to be alone with my brain.
And I have a Zoom class to teach in a few hours:
a black and white cat's back and forth in front of the camera,
meowing, meowing, meowing.

Writing needs silence.
I think of the woman who wrote her novels in a room full of
people,
of the black playwright who wrote his great plays in a bar,
of the Egyptian novelist who wrote his great novels in a bar.
Now the customer can pay extra to sit where he sat.
And me.
I need to be alone with the universe inside my head.
Meow, meow, meow.
Maybe tomorrow I will get to the grandson, the blue cake around
his mouth,
the family, 8 of us, singing "Happy Birthday."
Evren, grow up to do something big because
you have a wonderful world to be human in.

I taught Evren thumbs up.
I went thumbs up and for the first time in his life he copied
thumbs up.
So thumbs up.

These damn bites all over my arms, my neck, my butt.
I am one big itch.
What did I do to the bed bugs?
Nothing.
That's so human.
I didn't wrong them so they shouldn't wrong me.
Humans wrong people they don't know.
War, and bombs fall on total strangers, babies.
A man approaches someone in a parking lot, AR-15 out.
"Give me your car keys," he says.
But I don't know you.
Sounds stupid.
Spray the beds; kill the bugs, all of them.
Meow meow meow.
Della, shut up.
No treats for you.

Maybe tomorrow.
More on the first birthday
More on his sister running, dancing, flipping.
Just more
in the silence
with my brain.

September 20, 2022

No cat.
She tried, but I shut the door to the stairs in time.

Evren was 1 last weekend,
A cute, of course, boy with lots of black hair.
He crawls, he smiles, he claps.
I went thumbs up with him, and he imitated, thumbs up.
Actually, his was more thumbs sideways.
The whole family was there in St. Louis,
Jennifer, Grandjen as she is called, and me,
my ex-wife Debbie and Bob,
and Engin and Lamia, my daughter's husband's parents,
originally from Turkey but now in Minnesota.
"Evren, your name means 'the universe'", my daughter told the
birthday boy.
"That means you are the universe."
Birthday cake with blue icing so that Evren's mouth became
blue.
Singing "Happy Birthday" of course.
Allison, my 5-year-old granddaughter, exhausted Jennifer.
She wanted to dance, dance, dance.

Evren, 1 year old.
On to 2.
Soon he may be walking.
Soon he may be talking.
A new person to clap with.

September 21, 2022

Red splotches over my hands and neck.
One on my butt.
Bed bugs?
I think so, but the doctor thinks maybe poison ivy.
Don't see how that could be.
I have not been rolling in poison ivy,
but I have slept in a motel bed with one tiny dot of a bug.
My wife has a few splotches too from her bed,
we think.
I don't think I'm going to die, but I hope I haven't spread my
splotches
to my family,
celebrating Evren's first birthday in St. Louis.

At least the splotches are decorative.

Mortality.
Yet another title for my autobiography.
Years.
Another title.
Wild guesses,
yet another.

At least I don't live in an era of malaria, smallpox or black
plague.
Oh wait.
There's Covid, and now
monkey pox.
The planet isn't safe for humans,
though most of the danger comes from other humans.
Nuclear.

Automatic rifles.
Knives.
Cars swerving into the wrong lane.

I am keenly aware that several people hate me,
though I have done nothing to them.
Javaid, Peggy, Dale, Denise, Eddie.
It is hard to live with their hatred.
Hard to wake up and check my messages.
"Old fool".
"Old goat."
"No show Flynn."
Connecting with the community, other humans,
has been a given with me, I think.
Helping.
Well, maybe that's over.
The hackers, who send out horrible messages from my email, my
phone SMS,
have won.
So maybe something new.
Instead of the blues I will help with literacy.
No more president of the local blues or musicians aid societies,
no more director of all-day blues reunions.
One-on-one with someone who can't read or write.
I need a purpose.

Red splotches.

September 22, 2022

The dishwasher flooded the kitchen floor with water last night,
and there is a leak in the pipe under the sink.
We wait for the plumber.
So I am not wearing my noise suppression headphones,
and living in a world of silence.
Instead, I hear the air conditioner, I heard the keys on the key-
board,
I wait my wife telling me the plumber is here.
Stop writing, stop thinking, come on down.

September 23, 2022

I am writing to my brain.
Brain, here are words.
Mishmash.
Bivalve.
Nomenclature.
You are welcome.
A lot of what we think is abstract.
Sounds.
Systems.
Guesses.
The specific is secondary,
contained in the clouds.
Machine, coffee maker.
Shoes, these shoes on my feet.
People, her.
I don't believe birds are free.
I believe they work all day looking for food.
I believe they guard territory from other birds.
I believe they mate.
Belief.
Birds.
The woodpecker that tapped on my back wall this morning,
looking for mold, fungus, food.
Birds.

I don't want to fly.
I want to keep walking.
Good enough for me.
And driving.
And very occasionally sitting in a plane.

Flap flap flap.
Seems like a lot of sweat.

So what does all this amount to?
1.

September 24, 2022

New day, old everything.
My red bumps still itch.
The cat woke me up this morning so I am sleepy,
in a fog.
Finished one *The Economist*;
will start another one tomorrow.
The best I can say is
I am fighting for the same.
Better?
Maybe later.
Worse?
Maybe later.
Now a straight line, maybe black, maybe red, maybe white
so that it disappears on the screen.
Something fun.
That's what I need,
Something fun.
Not attacks on me.
Not itchy bumps.
Not same day same day same day.
A trip to
fill in the blank.
Cruising along the interstate,
listening to music from the 70s,
thinking.
No hacker messages.
Nothing broken down in the condo.
But something.
Confidence.
Feeling good about myself.
I have done a lot that is admirable.

Nobody cares, but it exists.
A goal, maybe my old home town,
maybe a tourist attraction like the Bell Witch Cave,
maybe a city, a different city from my city.
Then turn around, and drive back.
But that's O.K.
Just some sense that something exists other than new day old
day.

This is all so ordinary, so cliched.
But
it's what I've got.
You too?
I drink coffee from the black cup, and smile.
We are in this milk pool together.

September 25, 2022

Last night I dreamt about meditation,
and woke thinking that is what I will do come January
when my teaching load is not so heavy.
Meditate, turn off the world
with its hackers, its haters, and its hound dogs.
Maybe zazen.
Friends did that in Japan,
a week's training.
A line of them trying to be nothing.
If any one showed signs of consciousness,
like looking around,
the Buddhist monk would whack them over the head with a flat
bamboo bat.
Nothing.
Wouldn't it be great to be nothing for chosen periods of time, a
half hour say.
Sitting on my meditation mat,
eyes open but seeing nothing.
Thinking nothing.
Being nothing.
Now I am something and that's a target.
Of course there are other types of meditation.
People can't decide.
The last I read there were more than 20,000 official Christian
churches,
each thinking the others are going to burn in hell for eternity.
Same for Islam, same for every religion,
every system of thought,
every political belief.
Every.

In my dream I was married to a Japanese woman and we sat, legs crossed
in an empty room,
a Victorian empty room.
I can't do that,
but I can be married to my beloved wife,
and sit, legs out,
on the rug in my messy attic office
ignoring the piles of books,
the piles of paper,
the piles of wires and obsolete printers,
the world.
Thank you, brain, for the dream.
It showed me my future.

September 26, 2022

Terrible night last.
Wife mad.
"You're not a man."
The sink and dishwasher clogged again.
Life in its distracted, sharp pained way.
Which happens a lot.
So much of life is recovering when bad happens.
The clogged sink of creation.

September 27, 2022

Brain storm.
The sky grows darker and darker.
The wind blows the leaves of the forest.
Thunder drums the distance.
Then the sheet of rain hits the house.
Lightning blazes the living room.
The world outside turns white
with rain,
with lightning.
The furniture on the deck crashes into the railing.

Unlike an outdoor storm this one continues all day.
15 minutes and an outdoor storm moves on.
All day and the brain storm crackles and floods.

I am having a brain storm today, obviously.
Might just be a headache,
but might just be despair.
A cold front moves past in the brain sky.
Tomorrow, partly sunny,
below average highs and lows.
I'll make it.
Can't wait for the fall,
The red leaves.
The crisp air.
Cliché!
The aluminum foil air.
Early Christmas ads.
Football on TV.
Stew.

Rambling.
Brain storm.

September 28, 2022

I used to go fishing with my grandfather Roy on the Tennessee
River.
Now I let corporations do my fishing for me.
Frozen tilapia.
Frozen mahi mahi.
Scottish salmon in a plastic bag.
None of that in the Tennessee River.
Catfish with whiskers.
Bass.
Crappie (pronounced croppie).
We would take his boat,
a wooden one he built himself,
to our favorite spots.
There was a tangle of branches where the bass hung out,
for example.
Fish.
Put the fish in the live well of the boat.
And gather them for dinner.
My Uncle Ross once mailed me a package of raw bass.
From Jackson, TN, to Nashville, TN.
They arrived wet, stinking, and gross.
I cooked them nonetheless.
Didn't get sick.

Fish.

My daughter Caitlin was about three
When her goldfish died.
The goldfish floated lifeless on top of the aquarium in our living
room.
I had her take him to the toilet, we prayed, and ceremoniously

she flushed him away.
A few hours later I heard her scream from the bathroom.
There, floating on top of the water,
was her goldfish.
Resurrection?
I didn't want to go into that with her just then.
Still dead.
A second ceremony.
More prayers.
She flushed again.
This time the goldfish remained in heaven.

Flounder, swordfish, shark fin,
even whale.
I've had them all.

I was in a sushi restaurant, or rather a sushi place because it was
tiny,
just a counter,
near my apartment in Kawachinagano, Japan.
I sat on the stool while the chef prepared each piece of sushi.
Actually, the café was closed; it was past time and I was the
only customer.
The chef brought me another piece, like sashimi.
"Try this one, and tell me what it tastes like?" he said.
He almost looked angry.
I did.
It tasted like bacon.
I told him so.
"This is a part of the whale," he said self-righteously.
Whale was illegal in Japan at that time.
It had been a staple before the international community banned
whale meat,

wanting to save the creature.
Some Japanese still insisted it was part of the national diet.
A political stand.
The chef apparently was one of these.
He looked at me like I was the one banning whale,
and gave me a lecture on Japanese culture.

Once in Hawaii I was talking on the phone,
looking out my living room window.
I lived in a cottage on the hillside overlooking the Pacific Ocean.
A splash caught my attention in the far water,
not the usual splash.
I had bought a pair of binoculars
to watch the passing ships,
but I looked with those.
A whale, a humpback, jumped out of the ocean,
and splashed back in.
He, it did this several times.
Thank you, whale.
I still remember you decades later.
Hope you enjoyed the air.

So, to put all this together.
No, I won't.
Fish, whales, crabs, squid,
they are all separate from
my television,
the street in front of the condo,
the grocery store three miles away.
I want to keep them separate.
One system, blah.
Trillions and trillions of all.
Yeah.

Did I tell you about the time friends and I camped on a beach in
El Salvador,
and woke to dozens of crabs trying to tear down the tent?
Maybe next time.
Maybe.
There is so much.

September 29, 2022

That date is entirely artificial.
September: divide the year into 12s.
29: divide the months into 28, 30s and 31s.
2022: Elsewhere on the planet it is a different year: different
systems.

But we live by the clock.
For example, today I have an appointment for a haircut at 1:10
p.m.
Military that's 13:10.
I live by that schedule.
Wake up about 9 a.m.
on the clock on the table by my bed.
Watch the clock while I am writing,
so there are minutes left for shaving, brushing my teeth, eating
lunch.
Dress about 12:15 p.m.
Leave for the salon about say 12:45.
I live by numbers.
I am ruled by numbers.
So are you.

The numbers are totally different, say, on Neptune.
Sunrise, sunset?
Different.
Circle around the sun?
Different.
Life expectancy.
Probably different as well.

I expect to live another five years,
dying in 2027.
On average.

Other numbers that rule my life:
Only child: 1
Retired: 65.
Fingers: 10.
Nose: 1.
Eyes: 2.
Penis: 1.
Legs: 2.
Feet: 2.
Toes: 10.
Liver: 1.
Neck: 1.

So what I have to do is generalize so I can make it through a day:
1.
Not this step, this step, this step, out the door into another room.
But walk out the door into the other room.
I generalize
to exist.
So do you.

September 30, 2022

A month can seem a short time,
or it can seem a long time,
or it can seem an eternity.
So much trivia.
So much profundity.
New underwear.
Nearly dying in a near car wreck.
That was yesterday actually.
And a lot of softness, like hummus and a movie about a dog
dying.
Months are like . . .
I started but months are like everything,
Because everything takes place or is realized or is sensed
in some month.
These poems are one month's sample.
The interesting, the boring,
the sharp, the dull,
the idea and the object.
And more.
And everything.

Pretty obvious, isn't it?

So I want to feel better.
Thank you, Japan
for haiku,
which the following is not.
Senryu?

A yellow leaf falls,
and is swirled with other leaves.
I remember you.

October 1, 2022

October used to be my favorite month.
Cool, fall colors, long sleeves.
Now it can be hot, can be cold, can be dry.
The trees are still green although with a few yellow leaves.
It's spider mating season.
No cricket in the condo so far.
They were supposed to be good luck,
so I would gently catch them, and throw them outdoors.
None so far this year, good or bad luck.
I am cooking Irish Stew this Sunday, however.
Beef, and potatoes, and carrots, and onions.
Warms you inside.

Another year and another season.
But a hurricane has destroyed Florida,
and we are in a drought.
Fire danger in the woods out the windows.
Not much to celebrate, but then
when has there been much to celebrate.
Sounds whiny, doesn't it?
Whiny and diney.
That's me.

I can't be profound when my back hurts.
Sorry.
New month, new possibilities, old sighs.

October 2, 2022

Made it to another day.
Hi, day.
No answer.

I won't cure cancer.
I won't eliminate hunger.
I won't stop crime.
So what will I do with this day?
A small space: this chair, this keyboard, this screen, and down-
stairs
that sofa, that coffee table, that TV, that remote.
Elsewhere: my car.
That's all. I am a human.

So let's say I am Vladimir Putin.
I live in a billion dollar home.
I own a half billion dollar yacht.
I decide to invade Ukraine.
Thousands will die.
Babies by the hundreds will burn to death.
Millions of lives destroyed.
But I can do it, so I do.
Then what?

Cliché:
Humans are small.
We cure and we kill,
but so do ants.
We cure and we kill ourselves,
and ourselves are right in front of our eyes.

Trillions of galaxies, you know.
We aren't even grains of sand.

So today I accept my nanoness.
I accept my death, coming in a few years.
I accept my lack of profundity
or even my ability to be right.
I sit here, typing, a system I learned in high school
because I had a crush on a girl who was taking the same class.
QWERTY.
My key to the universe,
which is a cliche
too.
I ramble.
I stumble.
I strut, but only I know it.
I love life
but I know it is a quark
and not
a mountain.

October 3, 2022

I am sad.
Let's cope with that.
Sad throughout my body.
Sad in my brain.
Sad in my eyes.
What has been is sad.
What is is sad.
What will be is uninteresting.

So why don't I get out of this chair and scream "Dammit!"?
Fight.
Aim.
Scheme.
Produce.

Because I am sad.
What can I aim for that I haven't aimed for in the past?
Happiness?
No.
Success?
No.
Sainthood?
No.

Instead I will step through this day.
A theme it seems in these poems.
Step one step two step three.
Why?
I don't know.
Toward what?
I don' t know.

And I have stepped before.
Step one billion.
Step one billion and one.
Step one trillion.
So on.

So on.

October 4, 2022

I don't have anything to say.
So I'll say it.

A month is partial,
1/12 of a year,
1/120 of a decade.
But you knew that.
I'll shut up now.

No, I feel like talking.
Nothing to talk about,
but I'll talk.

A bird on the deck
stares at me through the window.
Curious about what?

I need to delete that.
So instead I will blabber
About quantum entanglement.
Scientists won a Nobel Prize for research in the field today.
Quantum entanglement is, say, two particles
far apart,
even the ends of the universe
unless the universe is curved
or one of many universes.
Change happens to one particle
and that
causes
change in the other particle
even though they aren't physically connected
As far as we know.

The scientists want to base a new kind of computer
on entanglement.
I want to base a new kind of
religion
on entanglement.
Entanglement is God.
That's a start; a whole theology can follow.
I'll see if I have the time.

I like words.
Words by themselves,
not racked in sentences.
Like, oh let's say,
embroidery.
Could be the design of all creation.
Maybe not.
But then
stacks.
Could be the design of all creation.
Maybe not.

I have a headache.
Could be the design of all creation.
I don't know.
You don't know.
They don't know.
I only have a few years left to figure this all out,
and know I won't.
So a word: camouflage.
Think I'll leave it at that.

October 5, 2022

A woodpecker pecked on the other side of the wall from my bed.
Woody?
Della the cat scratched and banged at my bedroom door.
So
no sleep.
Instead

I will dream awake.
I dream of adventure, a trip to South Africa, a return to Israel, a
return to the Amazon.
I dream of New York City,
walking, looking, talking, seeing.
I dream of music,
sitting in a bar with a Bud Light listening to a blues singer, male
or female,
revealing his or her soul
while the patrons talk loudly about stupid friends.

I dream of sleeping,
the woodpecker full of fungus or mold or whatever he or she
pecks from our outside wall.
The cat asleep in a cardboard box in the living room.
I dream of dreaming.

October 6, 2022

More woodpecker and cat.
I write this from far away.
My body is in this chair, my fingers on this keyboard, my eyes on this screen,
but my brain is in the mountains.
Oh hell, I'm just sleepy.

Death is coming.
Might be a year, might be five years, might be ten years, might be twenty years, might be,
heavenly horseradish,
thirty years.
Thirty years and I would be 104.
That would be an accomplishment,
Like completing a crossword puzzle.
Just more me.

I of course have no idea what happens after death.
Nothing
or
heaven, a house with walls of jasper, suns and angels,
or
hellfire and pain like the planet is on fire.
Or
something else.
I will have to wait.
Will get back to you if I can.

I have never seen a ghost,
But supernatural things have happened to me.
The Virgin Mary appeared by my bedside when I was about 13.

Her fingers touched my cheek.
I swear this happened,
swear on my soul.
A couple of weeks later the Sacred Heart appeared unmoving on
my bedroom wall.
It was a holy card I had gotten at school,
exactly the picture on the holy card.
Then when I left Denver one day before Christmas,
on my way to my parents' house in Tennessee,
a dog greeted me at the door to the school building.
I was going to drop off a term paper.
The dog was black.
I left by the back door.
The black dog waited there.
I drove across the plains of Eastern Colorado.
A two-story house was on fire.
Nobody was fighting the blaze.
Then I stopped for gas in western Kansas.
The attendant had a fire mark on his face.
Hours later I stopped for gas in Kansas again.
It was night, foggy, the plains still.
The attendant filled my tank and came to the window.
He had a fire mark on his face.
"I wouldn't go past Salinas if I was you. Don't go past Salinas."
That town was about a hour's drive more.
I of course went past Salinas,
to see what would happen.
Nothing.
Nothing happened.
And my friend Marion died.
She was The Queen of the Blues.
The mayor of Nashville had issued a proclamation years before.
I was in the hospital room when she died.

I entered and the spikes on the scope rose.
She knew I was there.
The doctor came in later, used his stethoscope,
and told us
"She's passed."
That night my wife and I went to bed.
On the chest of drawers was an electric candle.
The battery had died many months before and the candle had
been dark.
About 4 a.m. we both woke.
The room was ablaze with light.
The candle was lit.
It stayed lit for a half hour.
"Marion," I said. "Welcome."
"Take the candle into the garage," my wife begged, burying her
head below her pillow. "Get it out of
here."
The candle stayed.
It blazed for two more nights,
Then was dark.
I told a city councilwoman about this time and she said,
"Of course."

If I can come back as energy, light, a butterfly, any way, I will.
If not, keep struggling.
Remember me until your brain dies too.

Think I had better concentrate on life while I'm here.
Live until you don't.
That's my motto.
Hi, ghosts all around me in this room.

October 7, 2022

I am alone.
Everybody is alone.
8 billion humans alone.
Soon more.
So we connect.
Through language.
Languages, that is.
Sight, sound, all that kind of stuff.
My brain, my skull.
You are there.
I am there.
Julius Caesar is there.
Pop star is there.
Wittgenstein is there.
As is Ethiopia.
Country.
As is Europa.
Moon.
As is Engraved Hourglass.
Nebula.
As is brain.
Brain is in my brain.

No rain.
We are in a drought.
The leaves are dying.
Fire danger.
No firepits.
Dead grass.
All in my brain.
If fire, a message from outside.
Burn.

All of this doesn't mean much
unless I want it to
or unless it falls into my five senses.
A car crash.
Usually I just drive along the lanes of the interstate.
A tired truck driver swerves into my car.
Tumble and death.
But not today.
Out there,
beyond the walls of my condo,
someone dies because someone with a gun mistakes him for
someone else.
Etc.
Lots of stuff.
That's why I want to be a hermit.
I park at the grocery store.
A drug addict pulls a Glock on me,
Shoots.
Dead.
It's too expensive to be a hermit these days though.
How much does a cave cost?
Bills have to be paid.
A hacker sends me messages, posts a picture of me taken from
my phone's photo app.
TV.
Web news sites.
I know I could avoid the last two, but then what: sitting on the
sofa staring into space all day?
I want to be a hermit, but I can't, so I won't.
Will join
something.

TGIF

That's a marker in the dark and stormy sea.

October 8, 2022

A month. What is that?
30 days?
31 days?
28 days?
29 days?
Since I have a choice with this book I choose 31 days.
A little extra glimpse.

I regret not having written this book from when I was born.
Imagine every day in my life.
Imagine every day in your life.
You are there on the page.
It is there on the page.
And I could keep writing this day after day until I die.
Imagine.
Senility ramblings.
Alzheimer's narrowings.
Dementia denials.
Or sharp looking back,
wisdom in the sense of lack of wisdom.
Death as a constant subject
with no solution.

No.
Maybe another month later,
another year,
another glimpse.
The idea is to keep every day,
good,
bad,

incoherent,
distracted,
witty,
witless.
Whatever.
But I will edit this through,
correct misspellings (How do I spell Alzheimer's? Have to look
that up on Google.)
Fill in bits.
Delete bits.
But keep the days, the precious days.

Yeah, 31.
But not end on fireworks.
Not end on The End.
Just another day.
That's profound.

October 9, 2022

There are no straight lines in a life.
It's all zig zags, circles leading to other circles, tetrahedrons,
parallels,
and other complications.
I want an anniversary trip to New York.
Too much work for that.
Maybe next year.
Too much work for that.
Money?
Air fare has gone up a lot.
A hotel room on Manhattan costs hundreds and hundreds a night.
Dinner hundreds more.
Money is always a zig zag.
And more uncertainties: health, wife's work, Covid, guns, etc.
So maybe.
Happy 21st anniversary, dear.
M
And let's say a new suit.
Money, again.
Size. I've enlarged.
Style. Pin striped no longer good except for gangsters?
Cloth. Cotton, yawn.
Time to visit the store, a sales person who helps—
last one examined me in one of the dark suits and said,
"You look like a waiter."
I always thought neckties were strange anyway,
this strip of cloth tight around the neck and hanging down the
chest,
sometimes thin and sometimes wide,
regimental or flowers or ducks or red or anything.
Our togas.
Zig zags.

So today,
grade essays, shower, shave, grade essays, mail bill payment,
grade essays, read novel, drink wine, slide
into bed.
If all that really happens as planned.
Zig zags.

When I was a child I wanted to be a pirate, then a mailman.
My father wanted me to be a civil engineer then a worker in the
local textile mill.
He sent a battery changer to talk with about that profession,
being sure the looms were supplied.
My mother wanted . . . I'm not sure what.
I grew up to be an English teacher without money, ever, for
anything.
Writer too, free of charge.
Oh, and priest. When I was a child I also wanted to be a priest.
The old priest said he would instruct me because there was no
Catholic high school in the area
until I graduated and could attend a seminary.
He invited black parishioners from the local black Catholic
church to mass one Sunday.
The whites got up a petition to have the priest moved away.
My father, in the Knights of Columbus, was a leader of that.
The bishop removed the priest and sent a new one.
Handsome, young, drove a convertible, joined the country club
which we couldn't afford.
He wouldn't help me be a priest.
A non-Catholic high school, four years and I wanted the world
instead.
Got this teacher/writer gig instead.

Zig zags.
Like today.
Like my life.
Like human history.
aybe.

October 10, 2022

Another day.
Like another skin cell.
Like another hair.
Like another human.
Like another car.

I am not going to make today a climax for this book.
Even a climax is not a climax.
The male body begins making more sperm immediately.
On to the next climax.

So again I will choose the first thing that comes to mind:
No. Not that.
Not that either.
Strike three.

The Dark Ages.
Madcap Medievals.
Macaroni and cheese with crab.

And that is my life,
Random and restricted and repeating.
Something new?
Sky diving.
Not really new.
I mean I've been kayaking in whitewater.
I've lived in a war zone, Macedonia.
Make that two: Israel.
Sat next to a nail bomb there.
Didn't know it of course.
Beersheba bus terminal.

Army arrived; evacuated us to the other side of the parking lot;
Took the bomb which was in the next gate, a foot from where I
sat
in the open air,
to a vehicle and exploded it.
Back to the gate.
On to Jerusalem.

So not The End,
But an end.
Millions of ends.
And that's just me,
My illusions, my mistakes, my smiles, my meanderings.
Sounds egotistical. Your.
Good days writing; bad days writing.
I'd say this was a bad day writing.

I don't like this ending.

October 11, 2022

Plans?
Hah. What are those?

www.ingramcontent.com/pod-product-compliance
Lightning Source LLC
Chambersburg PA
CBHW020937160726
47993CB00007B/2824